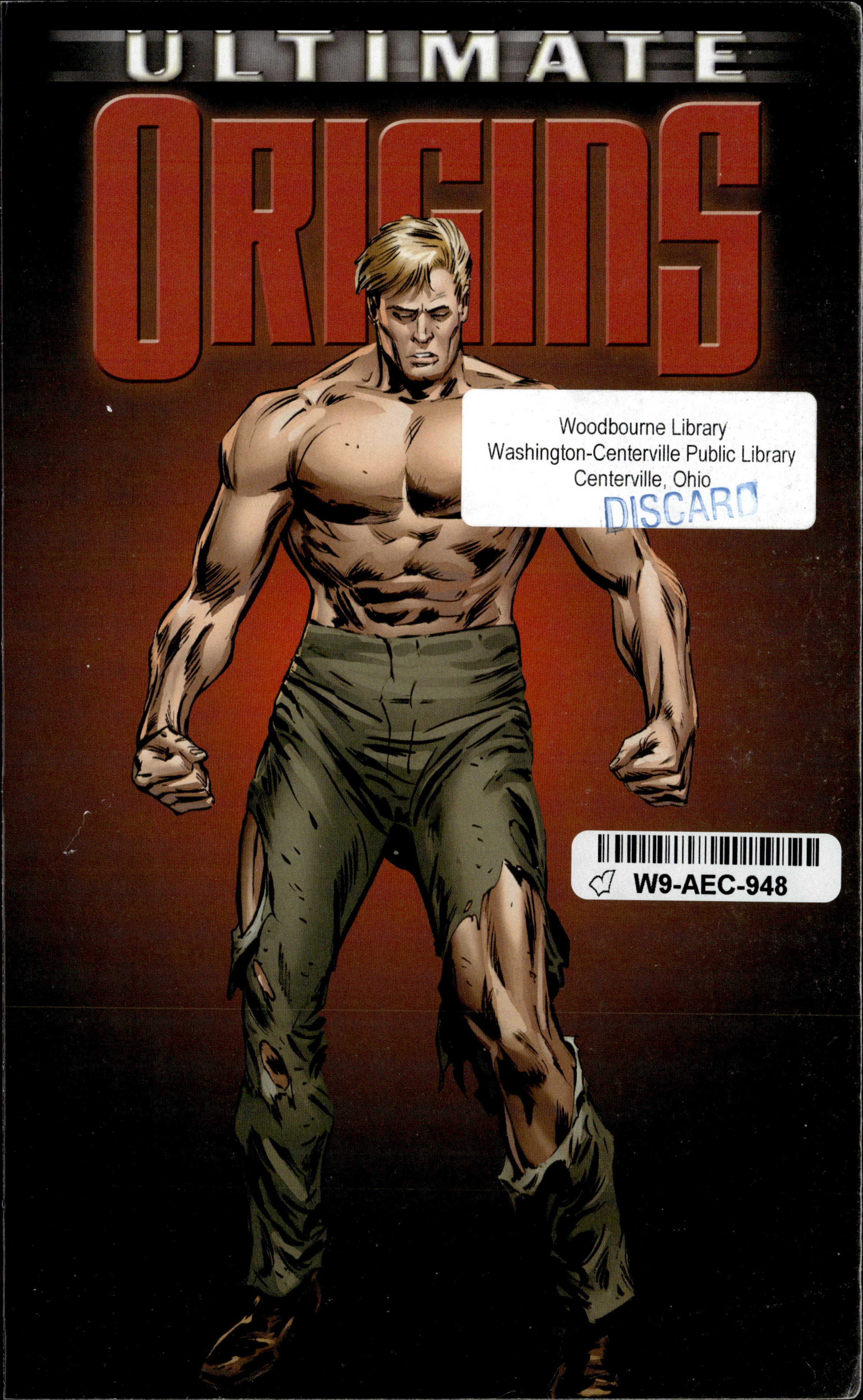
ULTIMATE
ORIGINS

ULTIMATE ORIGINS

WRITER
BRIAN MICHAEL BENDIS

ARTIST
BUTCH GUICE

COLORIST
JUSTIN PONSOR

LETTERERS
CHRIS ELIOPOULOS & VIRTUAL CALLIGRAPHY'S CORY PETIT

COVER ARTIST
GABRIELE DELL'OTTO

ASSISTANT EDITORS
LAUREN SANKOVITCH & LAUREN HENRY

EDITOR
RALPH MACCHIO

Collection Editor: Jennifer Grünwald • Editorial Assistant: Alex Starbuck
Assistant Editors: Cory Levine & John Denning • Editor, Special Projects: Mark D. Beazley
Senior Editor, Special Projects: Jeff Youngquist • Senior Vice President of Sales: David Gabriel
Production: Jerry Kalinowski • Book Designer: Spring Hoteling
Editor in Chief: Joe Quesada • Publisher: Dan Buckley

1 Variant Cover by Simone Bianchi

Manhattan docks, six months ago.
Listen, it's all connected.
That's it. That's the secret.
What is? Secret to what?
All of it- all of this- it's all connected.
You- me-
They don't want you to figure it out.
They don't want you to know.
Who are you?

Time to put on your collar, Doctor Banner.
Great! Where were you, like, a billion years ago?
Oh God! No!
LEAVE ME ALONE!
You know how this works, Banner-
You can either put it on yourself or I can put it on for you.
Wait- what is this? Who are you people?
Just leave me alone!!
Uh- why doesn't everybody just calm down a minute. Just-

You're interfering with a matter of...
...national security.
Oh no...

LEAVE--
What's going on?
ME!!
ALONE!!

FIRE!!

HHYYYAAARRRGGHH!!
BOOM
Oh man, target is on the move...
Repeat.
Target is on the move.
That's a negative on a direct hit, blackbird. That's a big, fat negative.
Yeah, we noticed.
Target confirmed.
The target is heading toward Jersey.
Pursue. The order is pursue.
Roger.

Guadalcanal Campaign
Battle of the Tenaru
August, 1942
WHUMP
WHRAM

TAKE THIS FIGHT RIGHT TO THEM, BOYS!!!

THIS IS FOR OUR FREEDOM!!
BWEE
KPOW
ZIP
RATATA
VIP
ZING
<What is that?>
<I don't know.>
<Aim for it.>
SPLAT
SPAT
VIP
VIP
BWEEE
POW
Let's show these ye-
VIP
BLAMBAM
TZING
VIP
ZIP
ZIP
TZIIING

This is terrible.
We *did* take the island, Mr. President.
Our super soldier is dead.
There's blood on the flag.
Well, sir, he was a good soldier.
But he was just a soldier.
Sir, you asked us to create a symbol-
I want a super soldier who really *is* a super soldier.
More than a man, he has to be a symbol.
A God-fearing symbol to those godless bastards.
Sir.
This is a war of images, gentlemen. Cameras and film...
I don't want to see *this*- I don't want to see a man in our blood-soaked flag lying on the bodies of those who died for our freedom.
Yes, sir.

The Allied Invasion of Sicily
August, 1943
WHUMPF

Makin' some noise there, Howlett.
Worked, dini't.
Hot diggity damn!!

So whadda we do now?
Hey Fisk, you say you know a guy who can move this stuff?
Uh, no, Fury. I ain't said that..
So whadda we do with it?
Split it up. You take yours, ship it home, stick it in your locker...

You think this is *real?*
It's in a safe, ain't it?
Well, it *was!*
Hahaha!!
What's this, now?

We're at war!
The freedom of the world is at stake!!
And this is what you do?

Private Nicholas Fury. Where's your unit? Do you even know??
(Told you it was too loud.)
Um, I'm just a Canadian soldier and I was just-
#$%#!!

Halt!
AAAGGHH!!
BAM

AAAGGHH!!

Whoa!!
Get off!!!
Settle down, midget!
SPOK
Ubersetzstelle
LE MESSINA

You know where we are?
Were you overseas?
Nope.
Yeah.
It was a long boat home.
Yeah.
What you in here for?
I don't think we're getting our day in court.

MP

This one.
Where am I?!!
Settle down, boy.
What is this??
Back away from the door.
Who are you?
Where *am I*?

Test subject 41. Project Rebirth.
Subject name: Nicholas Fury.
What is this?
The blood samples were healthy and matched that of subject 22, which had our largest success.
Please just tell me--
We've adjusted the plasma levels to match the previously taken blood sample.
We're hoping that the new mixture will bring a breakthrough.
Are you taking notes?
Yes, sir.
Just tell me what-!!!!
Pipe down and take your medicine.
This will be over momentarily.
It's in your best interests to relax and allow us to do our work.
I just- please!!! I just want to know what this is-
You wouldn't understand so it wouldn't help us to explain any of this to you.
Where am I?
You're in a laboratory and you've been selected for experimentation.
What kind of-??!!
It's an honor. I hope you know that.
Agh!
Injection successful.
Time 4:11 PM.
Time logged.
WHAT YOU DOIN' TO ME?!!

No protuberances.
Hmmm... that *is* promising.
Take his temperature.
How do you feel?

Open, please.
Mmm!!!

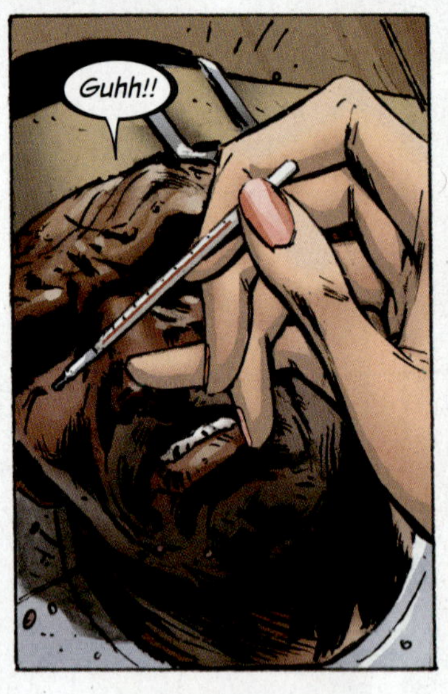
Guhh!!

NNYYAAAGGHH!!

Stations, everyone!!
Oh my God!!

NNYYAAAGGHH!!
NNYYAAAGGHH!!
CRAASH
Doctor??
Everyone hold formation.
Doctor??
MP

CRACK
Take it down!!
THUMP
Gah!
WOK
Argh!
BRIIIPP
THUNK
THWOP

BRIPPPP

Oh my God!!
Doctor??
Wh- where is he??
Did you put him down?
He- he let all the other prisoners go.
There're two teams on the ground still looking for him.
Please do try to find him.
Frankly I'd like to thank him. We finally have what we need.
We have our breakthrough.

Alberta, Canada
October, 1943
Let's wake him up.
NNYYAARRGGHH!
Settle!!
Stand down!!
Guns down.
You're with friends, James.

HURRAAGGH!!

Hugh!!
Hugh!
Hugh!!

Fan out.
Rocco seven.
X station--we have him. Orders?

Shoot him.
Shoot to kill?
You have your orders.

BRIPPPPPP

Target down.
Is he alive?
He's not breathing.
Double-check.
Yes, sir.

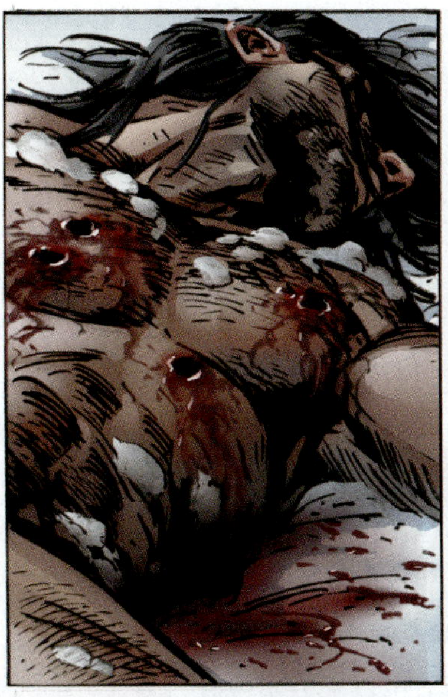

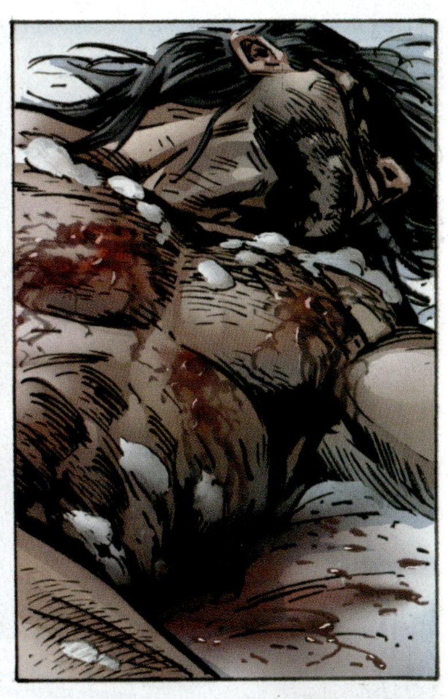

Whoa!!
Uh- did you guys see that-?
Grab him and bring him in before he wakes up.
Wakes up?
We shot him in the head.
The wounds- the wounds-
Bring him in quickly.

"I need you to explain this, Doctor Cornelius."
"I'm sorry this is such a shock to you. I thought we were on the same page."
"Just- just explain what you've done here."

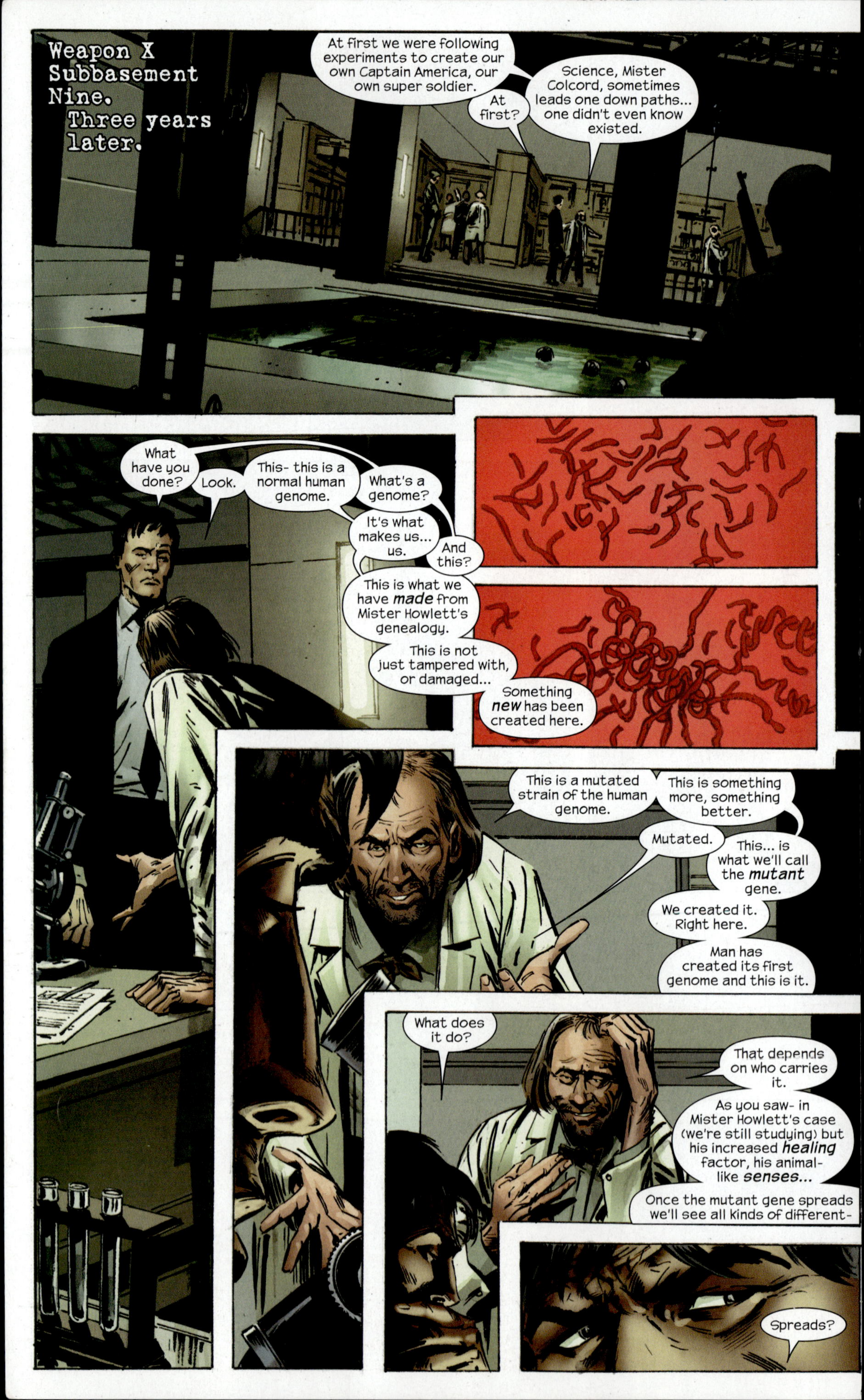

Weapon X Subbasement Nine. Three years later.
At first we were following experiments to create our own Captain America, our own super soldier.
At first?
Science, Mister Colcord, sometimes leads one down paths... one didn't even know existed.
What have you done?
Look.
This- this is a normal human genome.
What's a genome?
It's what makes us... us.
And this?
This is what we have *made* from Mister Howlett's genealogy.
This is not just tampered with, or damaged...
Something *new* has been created here.
This is a mutated strain of the human genome.
This is something more, something better.
Mutated.
This... is what we'll call the *mutant* gene.
We created it. Right here.
Man has created its first genome and this is it.
What does it do?
That depends on who carries it.
As you saw- in Mister Howlett's case (we're still studying) but his increased *healing* factor, his animal-like *senses*...
Once the mutant gene spreads we'll see all kinds of different-
Spreads?

Who knows how it will affect the others, but-
How will it spread?
Eventually man would become extinct. You do know that, right?
Like the dinosaur before him.
This never-ending world war might be our version of natural selection.
The beginning of our end.
But- but!!
Instead of finding a way to kill each other faster...
We have found a way to survive ourselves.
We'll survive, we'll evolve...
Right here- we control the fate of man.
We created a new species.
We've created the mutant.
And James Howlett...
Is mutant zero.

WHite

2 Variant Cover by Simone Bianchi

Project Pegasus.
Devil's Point, Wyoming.
Today.

Here we go.

Uh, hi.
Morning.
I'm Captain Carol Danvers. Acting director of S.H.I.E.L.D.
I brought the Fantastic Four because a couple of them are super brainiac big brains.
Say hi, super brains.
Hi!
(Johnny, believe me when I say she ain't talkin' about *you.*)
(Could be.)

Uh, where's Nick Fury?
Not here.
You might want to check your e-mail, Agent. There've been some memos.
Uh, where are the Ultimates?
The Fantastic Four are better suited for this.
Uh, who are you again?

There was a distress call. We're here to relieve that distress. Agent...
Wendell Vaughn.
Project Pegasus Director.
Yeah.
Project Pegasus is not something I knew existed 'til about an hour ago.
Yes, it's- it's top secret.

Yes.
Where's Nick Fury?
Why don't you show me what the problem is.
Um- it's top...
...secret.
Uh... okay. Follow me.

This is Project Pegasus.
What?
Is it like a museum?
It's where S.H.I.E.L.D. keeps all objects of mysterious origin or unexplained power that the United States authorities have accumulated over the years.

You keep all these objects in one place?
Dear Lord.
Obviously every precaution is taken to keep the objects safe.
Yes, but...
Hey, I didn't invent the place.

I, uh, I wouldn't touch that.
All these things- are there files on all of this??
Not for the public. And not on everything, no.
Nick Fury just threw anything he didn't understand into a mountain and hoped for the best??
This place dates back waaaay before Nick Fury's time.

Okay, well...
As hard as it is to imagine something could go wrong in a place like this...
What went wrong?? What's the emergency?

Well, that...

What is it?
I don't know.
But it was just sitting there, for, well, decades, and this morning...it-it *turned on.*
Richards?
Susan?
Um....
Is it *lookin'* at us?

New York, 1942.
The world at war and we take you there.
Hitler's armies goose-step toward Berlin as a reign of godless terror sweeps across Europe.
American troops come by boat, by plane, and by the thousands...
While here at home, the women do all they can.
Here we see American soldiers firing at German paratroopers just past the battlefield line...
Our President shakes hands with heroic soldiers wounded in the call of duty.
Vice President Truman is at the christening of a new battleship called the Defender of Tomorrow.
Meanwhile, Adolf Hitler addresses his masses calling for a strong and mighty end to the nations who threaten their--
Steve?
Steve Rogers?

Hey, Gail.
Are you here by yourself?
Umm...
This is- hey, this is a friend of mine from school. This is Stevie Rogers.
This is Patrick Loika. He just enlisted. He's shipping out.
Yeah, hey there.
Where've you been?
Oh, I'm... I'm working at the--
We should get together.
Sshh!!
Yeah, sure.
I mean it.
Doll, the movie's on. You're talking.
A hospital ship, with United States Army nurses...

...arrives in Port Moresby, to care for the troops wounded in the furious fight for New Guinea.

The more serious cases are sent back to the Australian mainland...

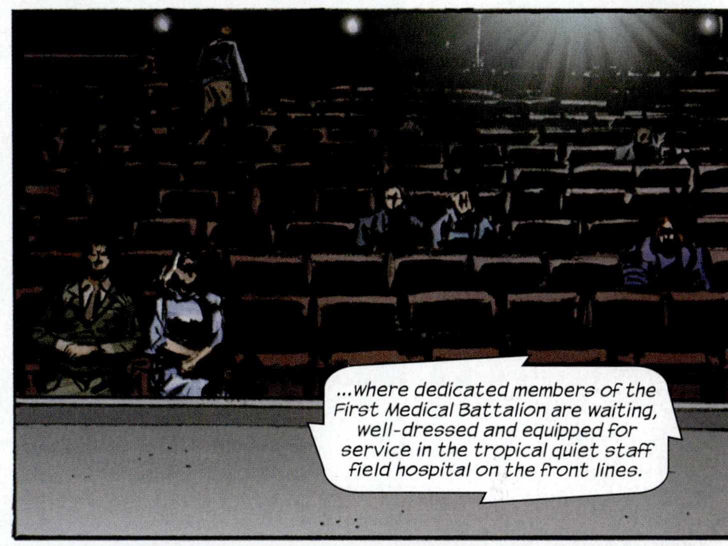
...where dedicated members of the First Medical Battalion are waiting, well-dressed and equipped for service in the tropical quiet staff field hospital on the front lines.

BERGMAN

WANT Y
How many times we got to go through this, kid?
U.S. AR
IST NO
Isn't there something I could do?
Kid, you *failed* the physical.
That means you ***stay here.*** You work at the factories.
With the ***dames??!!***
We all gotta do our part.
ED STATES
CENT
YOU

I- I could do ***your*** job.
Kid...
No, I ***could.***

Kid, I'm eatin'.

I ***want*** to do my part!!
I want to help stop this war. You tell me what to do and I'll do it.
I hear ya kid. I do.
No, you--
But I don't make the rules and the rules say you ain't fit for combat.
BRRING
You... you'd be a--

Yes?
Uh, okay.

Um, go in there.
Why?
Just go in there.
What's in there?

Mister Rogers, I'm Sergeant Dugan. Can we have a word?

Am I in trouble?
No.
What's this?
We wanted to talk to you about your predicament.

How many visits to the recruitment office has this been?
I'm...I'm sorry if I've been a pest. I only--
No one is angry with you, Steven.
We want to talk to you about your *passion.*

Why do you want to enlist so badly?
Why? Because... because the Germans and the Japs are wrong and they're going to take over the world if we don't stop them.

After you...

What is this place? Who are you?

My name is Sergeant Dugan of the United States Army.
My job, to be blunt, was to find *you.*
Please...there's someone who is dying to meet you.

I feel like I'm in *trouble.*
I promise you, you're not.
We've had our eye on you, Steven.
Orphaned... gimpy leg... patriotic... smart.
After your third trip to the recruitment office, we pulled your file.
I have a *file?*
Everyone has a file, kid. We're at war.

You *fit.* You're a perfect candidate. So we--
Perfect candidate for *what?*
Steve Rogers, I'd like to introduce you to...

...Doctor Erskine.
He runs Project: Rebirth.
May I have some blood and urine?

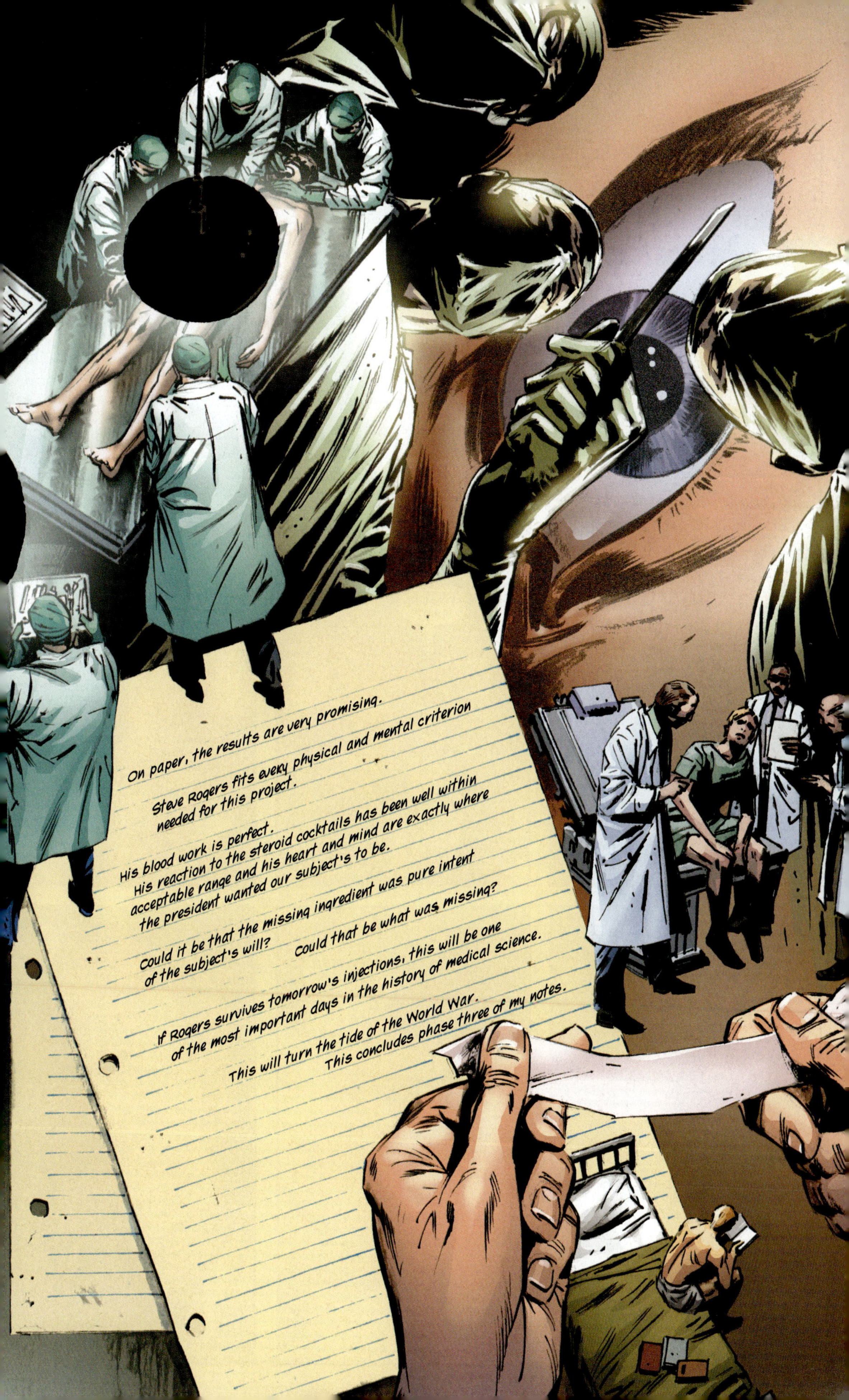
On paper, the results are very promising.
Steve Rogers fits every physical and mental criterion needed for this project.
His blood work is perfect.
His reaction to the steroid cocktails has been well within acceptable range and his heart and mind are exactly where the president wanted our subject's to be.
Could it be that the missing ingredient was pure intent of the subject's will?
Could that be what was missing?
If Rogers survives tomorrow's injections, this will be one of the most important days in the history of medical science.
This will turn the tide of the World War.
This concludes phase three of my notes.

How are you feeling, Steven?

I threw up this morning.
I'm okay now.
Did you?
You have a lot of chemicals in your system- it's nothing to worry about.
I'm ready, though. I'm ready.

You'll be ready soon. You have more reading to do.
What is this?

This is everything the American government knows about people who live on this planet that were not *born* here.
What?

On top of the Nazis and the Japs, you're going to learn that there are those working *with* them that are not from here.
Obviously we assume them to be the *most* dangerous and immediate threat.

What?
Little *green men* from *outer space?*

No.

Test subject 55. Project: Rebirth.
Subject name: Steve Rogers.
How are you feeling, Steven?
I'm ready.
That's good.

Have a seat.
Okey dokey...

Vital signs normal.
Blood work is stable.
Hi.

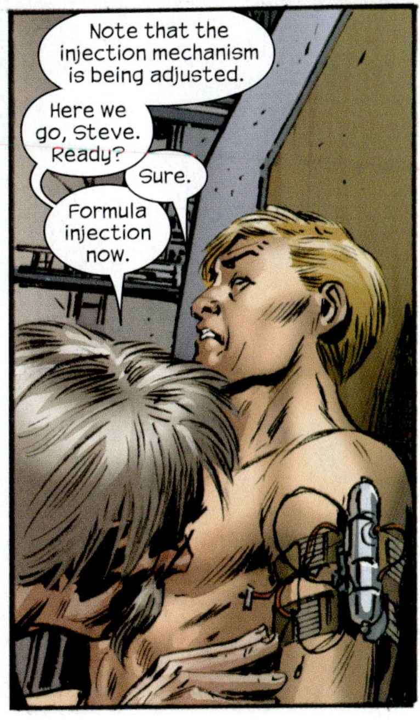
Note that the injection mechanism is being adjusted.
Here we go, Steve. Ready?
Sure.
Formula injection now.

Injection successful.
Time: 3:32 PM.
AGH!
Time logged.
Nn...
No protuberances.
Take his temperature.

How do you feel, Steven?
Nnaagh...

Vital signs within acceptable range.
(Write that down.)

Are you having trouble breathing?
I think... I am.

Check his pulse manually.

NNYAAAGGHH!!!
NNYAAGH!
Jeez!
Here we go again! On my order.
Hold on!!
HOLD ON!!!

Heil Hitler!
BAM

AGH!!
AGHH!!
BLAM
NO!!!
BAM
BLAM

SPTANNG!
Agh!!
KRRASH
NO!!
Oh, no!!!
No no...
Medic!! We need!!
We need a MEDIC!!
The hell is that?

Let's go! Go!!
You have to get *out of here!!*
What *is* that??
It might be a bomb!! *Go!!*

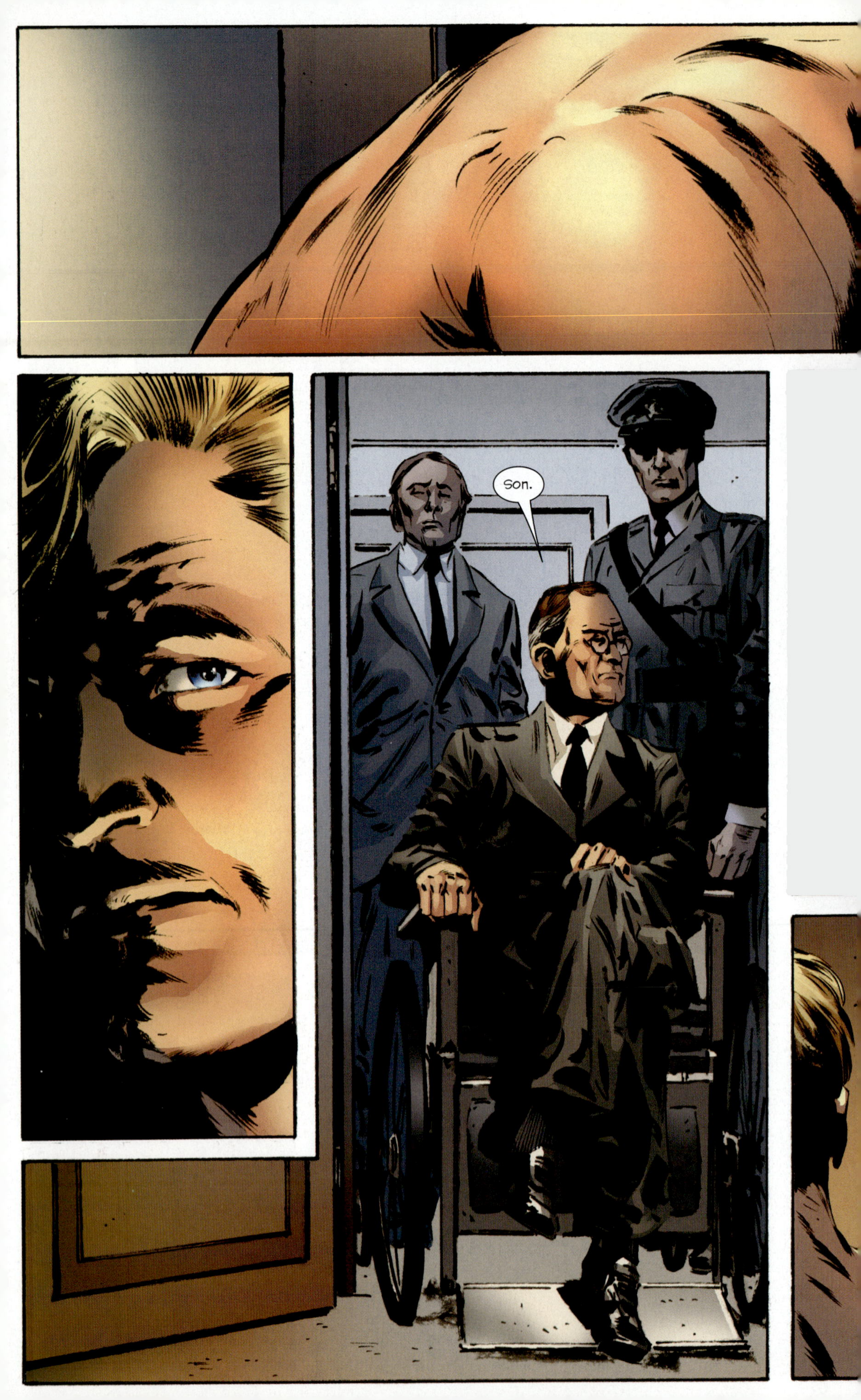
Son.

Mister President.
At ease, son.
I'm- I'm-
I know who you are. I'm here to see you.
I'm sending you overseas, son. I *have* to. We *need* you.
Yes, sir.
But there's... there's a lot going on that I don't understand.

I know, son. There's a lot to take in.
Plus, you're one of a kind now. The Nazis saw to that.
It'll take... I don't know how long to figure it all out again.
The doctor's notes- they're *incomplete,* they say. It was half in his head.
But- I wanted you to hear it from me...
You have to help us win this war.

I'll do my best.
Son, that's not enough.
Best. Good intentions. It's not enough.

You have to wear our flag and win this war.
Because without you out there, the *next* thing we'll be forced to do is *drop a bomb* on a country...
A bomb that kills... *everything* in it.
Every woman and child.
We'll have to commit *genocide,* son.
And I just can't have that on my soul.
See, I didn't start this war, I didn't want to be *in* this war, but by golly, I am going to end it.

Are you going to help me do that?
Yes, sir.

Hey, doll, you're late, you know.
It's not gentlemanly to keep a girl waiting.

I'm sorry, Gail.
What's the matter?
I'm shipping out.

Oh my!
Well, we knew this was coming.
Yes.
Doesn't make it any better now though.
No.

I love you, Gail.
I've loved you since middle school and I didn't have the guts to tell you.
I didn't- I don't know why. Now it's so easy.
But I *do.* I love you.

I love you too.

You don't need to say that.
It's true.
I didn't know that.

You're a hell of a gal.

When I get back...
I'd like to--

Say it when you get back.
Uh...
When *are* you coming back?

"When I'm done."

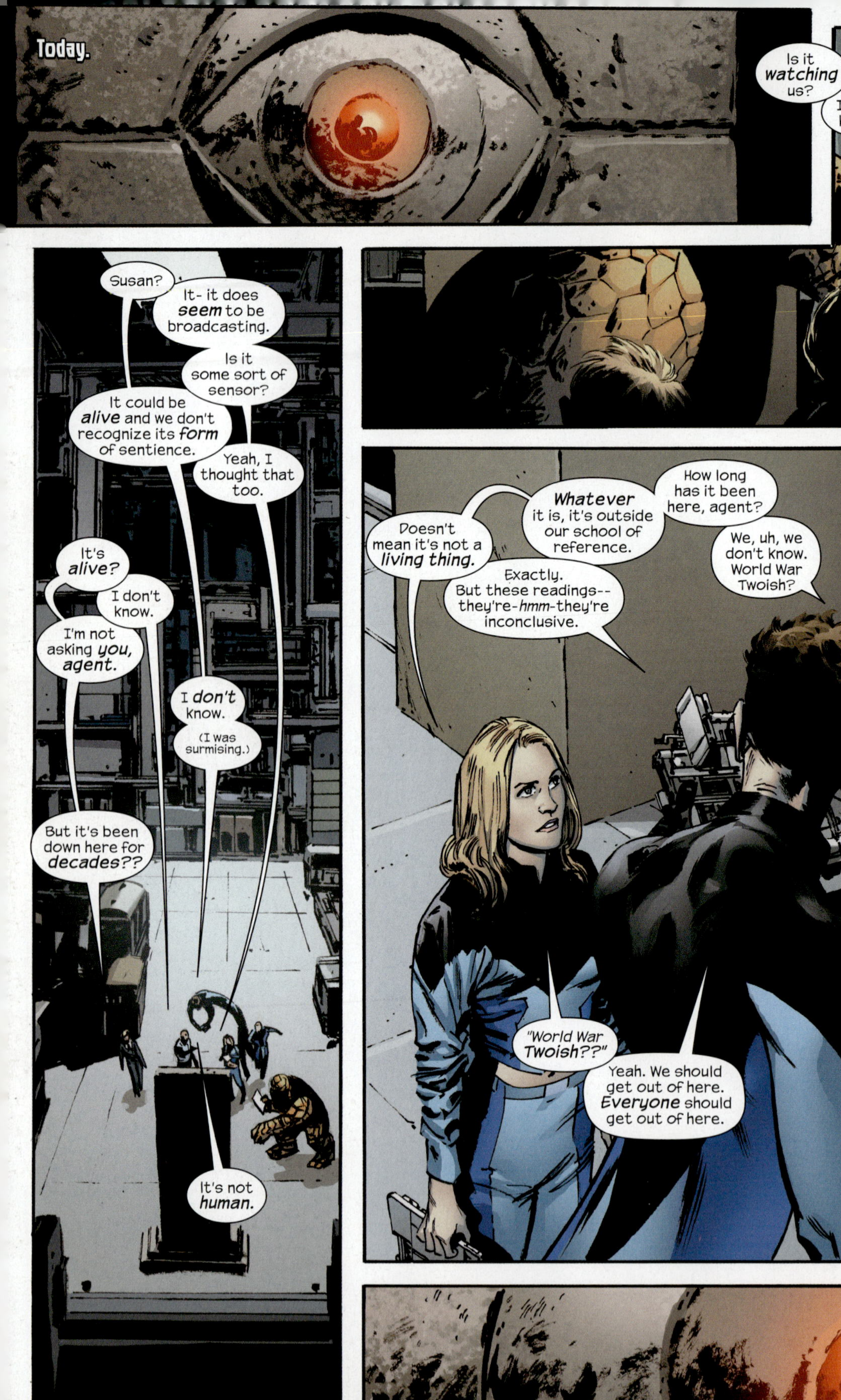
Today.
Is it watching us?
I don't know.
Susan?
It- it does seem to be broadcasting.
Is it some sort of sensor?
It could be alive and we don't recognize its form of sentience.
Yeah, I thought that too.
It's alive?
I don't know.
I'm not asking you, agent.
I don't know.
(I was surmising.)
But it's been down here for decades??
It's not human.
Doesn't mean it's not a living thing.
Whatever it is, it's outside our school of reference.
How long has it been here, agent?
We, uh, we don't know. World War Twoish?
Exactly. But these readings-- they're-hmm-they're inconclusive.
"World War Twoish??"
Yeah. We should get out of here. Everyone should get out of here.
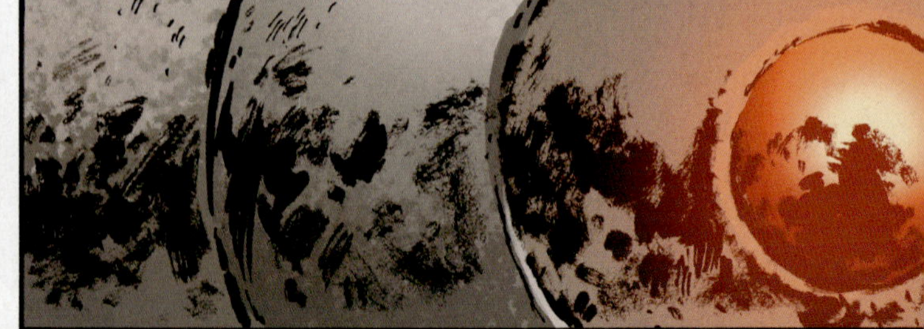

Project Pegasus, Wyoming.
Exact Location Unknown.
Why?
All of the technology created during the war was weapon-based, because, well, we were--
At war.
Exactly.
That's a weapon?
Or a bomb.
Or confiscated from the enemy...
Or alien technology that was being used as a weapon...
An alien bomb?

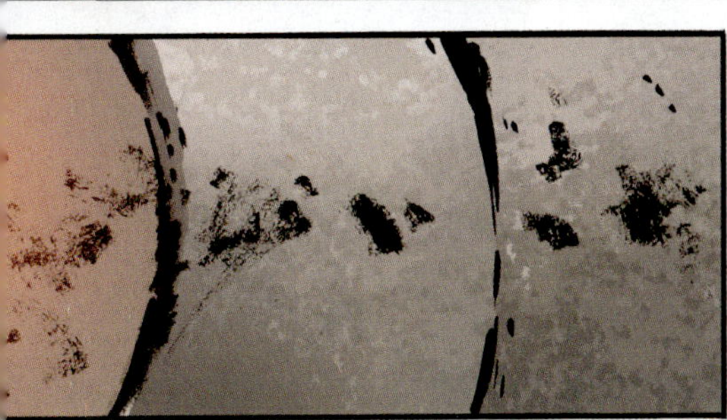

Yeah, uh...
Everybody out.

Okay, I want that thing in there *removed!!*
Like, from the *planet!!*
Um, I wouldn't do that, Director Danvers.
Okay. I want it- I want it- what do I want?
You want a team of experts down here to take readings.
You want to find out who put it here and why.
You want to find out if it's radiating any type of energy or virus that is hazardous to--
Yes!! I want ANSWERS!!!
Vaughn. There's a trail of paper that leads to this and how it got here, find it or go home.
'Cause *now* I'm scared that a horde of alien warriors is going to pour out of it or that it's going to melt the gonads of every man on Earth.
(Yeah, that's a good one too.)
DIRECTOR DANVERS!!
Busy!!!
It's important.
What's more important than *this?*
Well...

Tony Stark's Mansion, Home of the Ultimates.
Uh, guys?
Triskelion, S.H.I.E.L.D. Headquarters.
SECURITY BREACH--CODE ALPHA THIS IS NOT A DRILL!! SECURITY BREACH--CODE ALPHA THIS IS NOT A DRILL!! SECURITY BREACH--CODE ALPHA THIS IS NOT A DRILL!!
XAVIER'S SCHOOL FOR GIFTED CHILDREN

The Baxter Building,
Home of the Fantastic Four.
%@#$!!
Daily Bugle.
You were supposed to write a story about where Nick Fury is!!
And I got this instead, which is not--
YOU'RE FIRED!!
I'll sue you!!
London.
BBC
Brian Braddock has picked up two plum mounts in the big jumping races at Trentham on Saturday.
Hell's Kitchen.
Forest Hills, Queens,
Peter Parker's Attic.
Jazzy John's
PIZZA
AGH!!

Uh, guys?
Oh man...

Alberta, Canada.
27 Years Ago.
Get up.

NNYYAARRGGHHHHHH!!

AARRGGHHH!!
I know.
What they did to you.
NNYYHHHH!!
Your name is James. *James.*
Not Weapon X, not Mutant X.
James.
Do you know that? Do you remember?

HHHRRR!!!

I know.
It's over now.
You're free.

NNYARGGH!!
Erik, please!!

Please, Erik!!
This isn't how to do this.
This- This isn't your place.

Mother...
You look scared. Are you scared of me?

I am right now, Erik. Y- yes.
Put- put everything back and- and- and just calm down.

Your life's work is to torture this man.

My life's work is to help them find a cure--

For me.

For all of you.
You have a disease.
I'm trying to help cure--

Good bye, Mother.
I hope there is a hell.

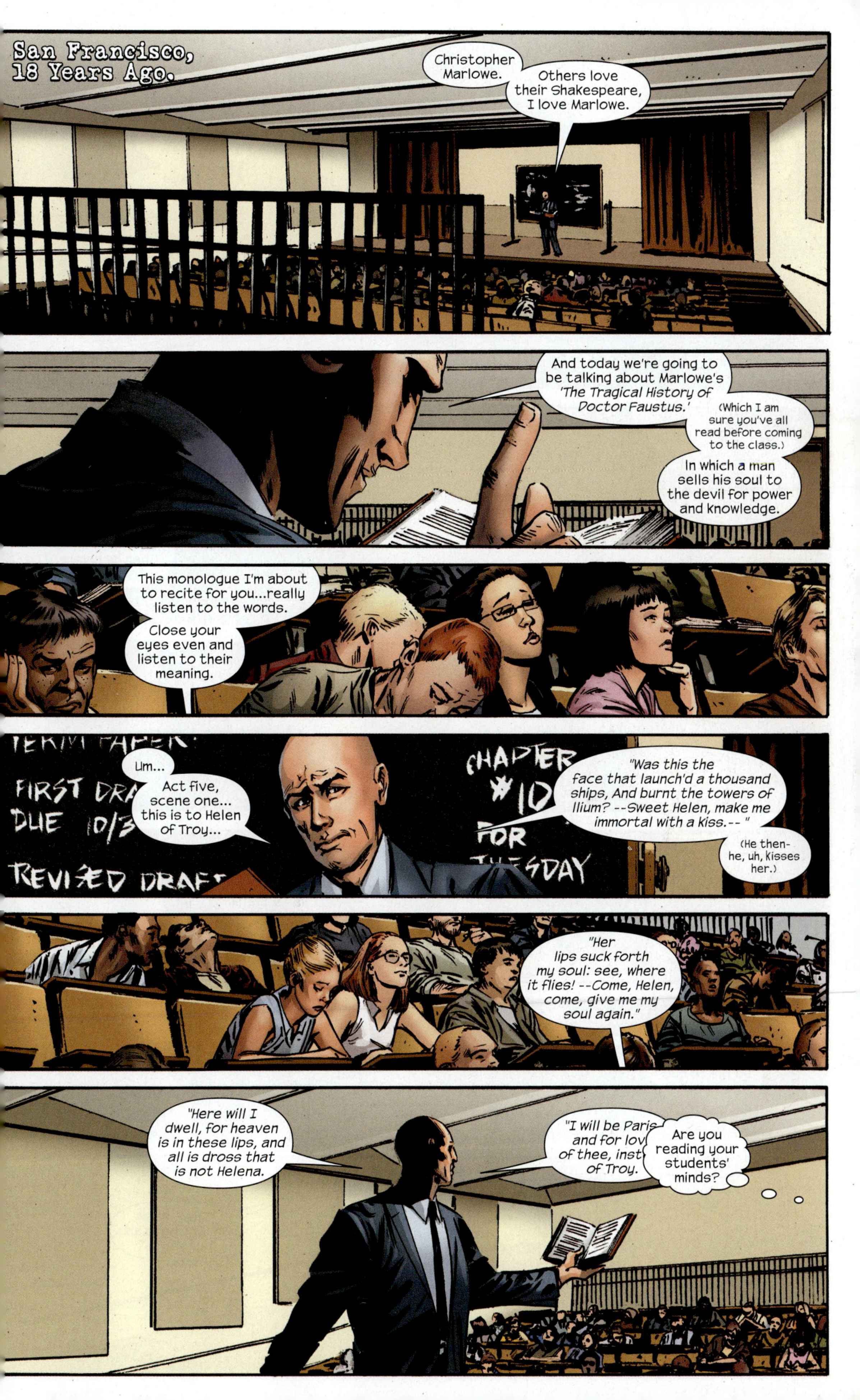

San Francisco, 18 Years Ago.
Christopher Marlowe.
Others love their Shakespeare, I love Marlowe.
And today we're going to be talking about Marlowe's *'The Tragical History of Doctor Faustus.'*
(Which I am sure you've all read before coming to the class.)
In which a man sells his soul to the devil for power and knowledge.
This monologue I'm about to recite for you...really listen to the words.
Close your eyes even and listen to their meaning.
Um...
Act five, scene one... this is to Helen of Troy...
"Was this the face that launch'd a thousand ships, And burnt the towers of Ilium? --Sweet Helen, make me immortal with a kiss.-- "
(He then-he, uh, kisses her.)
"Her lips suck forth my soul: see, where it flies! --Come, Helen, come, give me my soul again."
"Here will I dwell, for heaven is in these lips, and all is dross that is not Helena.
"I will be Paris and for lov of thee, inst of Troy.
Are you reading your students' minds?

"Shall Wittenberg be sack'd.
"And I will combat with weak Menelaus, And wear thy colours on my plumed crest.
Isn't that a tad unethical, Charles?
Though it probably does take the edge off dating them.
Takes out the guess work.
in the heel.
Who are you?
return to He
for a kiss.
Why can't I read inside your mind?
thou art
the evening
the beauty of
and stars.
"Brighter art thou than flaming Jupiter When he appear'd to hapless Semele.
I don't know.
That's interesting.
You can hear my thoughts to you but you can't look inside my mind?
"More lovely than the monarch
in wanton
's azur'd
Who are you?
"And none
thou s
pa
My name is Erik. I'd like to buy you lunch.
Okay, does anyone have any questions?

I read your book.
Well, that would be one of you.
To say I enjoyed it would be an understatement, Charles... it- it *moved* me.
Really?
You're surprised.
I *am* surprised.
Wasn't the point of it to move mutants to better their unique condition?
I thought- I thought it would have a little more impact than it did.
What was your print run?
I'm sorry. *Who* are you?
My name is Erik Lehnsherr. I am a mutant as well.
How did you know I was reading minds back there?
I can *always* tell when a mutant is using their manifestation.

Is that *your* manifestation?
No, actually.
What is it?
Magnetic fields.

Really?
Really.
I'd like to see that.

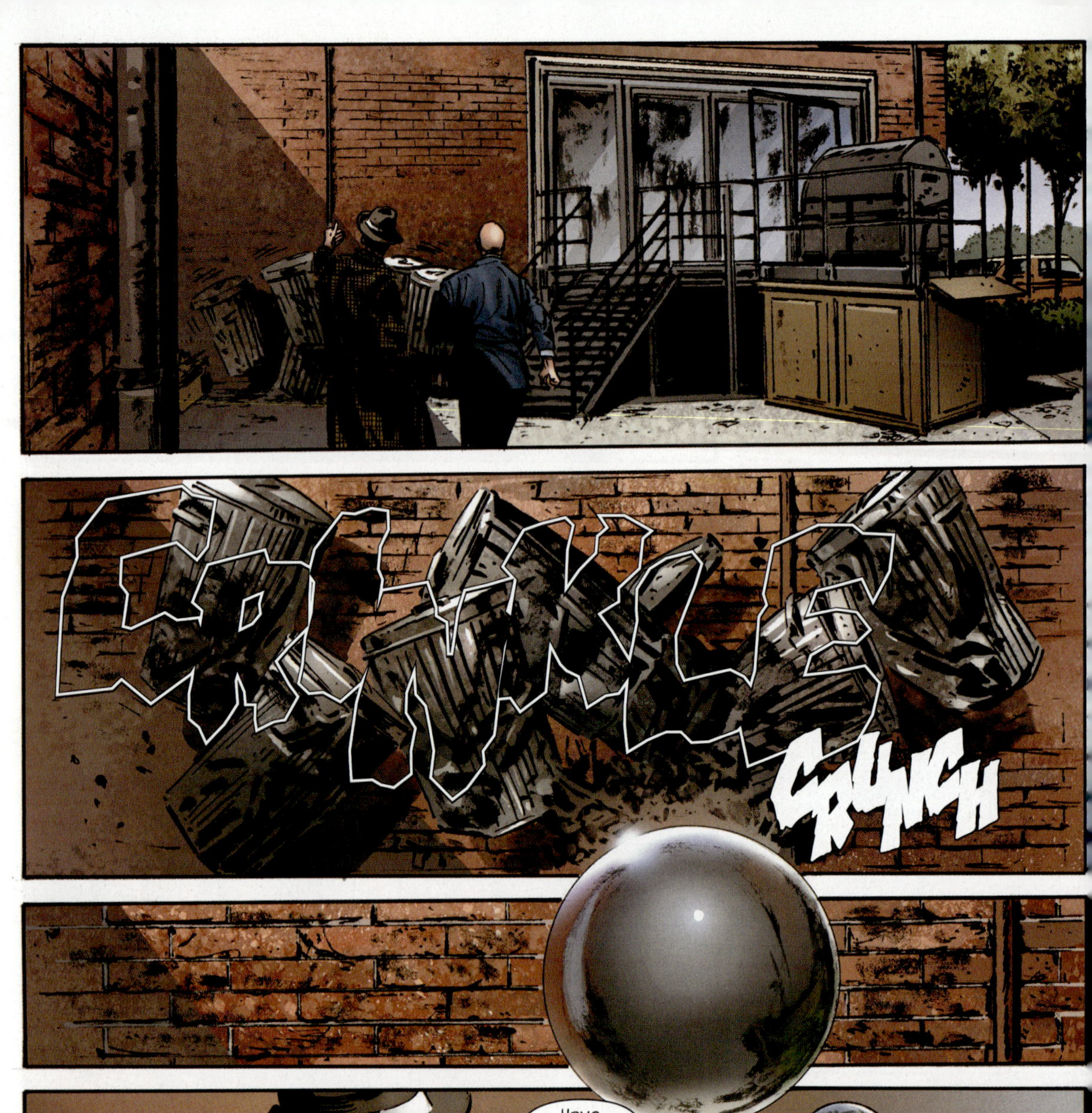
CRUNCH

Have you tested yourself?
Informally.

Why can't I read your mind?

I really don't know.
Maybe our powers *contradict* each other. That really intrigues me. We should examine that.
You're not blocking me out?
How would I do *that?*

I don't know.
You've never met anyone like me before?
Whose mind I could not get into? Not that I know of.

How about now?
No.
But you can hear me *think?*

Yes, but you're projecting that thought to me. It's like talking.
Sorry.

Actually. It's quite nice.
It's a nice change of pace.
I usually know the end of the conversation- or the true *intentions* of a conversation *before* the conversation actually happens.
This- I don't know who you are or *what* you're going to say.

I'm going to say that my friends and I were profoundly moved by your book.
And I thought your ideas of a place where mutants can gather and train...
Cultivate their race...
I *loved* this idea.
I want to make that *happen.*

Oh, okay.
Do you have a billion dollars?

No.
I have something better.

16 Years Ago.

A hundred times.
I know.
If I get to come here a hundred times.
I know.
Heaven on Earth.

Aaaah, the Savage Land.

Proof there's a god.
Yes.
But--
--is it *too* far away?

Charles, Charles, Charles...
Come meet your students.
A lot has changed since you were last here.

Our Brotherhood.
Can you feel how excited they are to see you?
They have gathered to do exactly that which you have written.
Brothers. Charles thinks we have removed ourselves from the fight.
No. No.
That's not what I said. I just wondered if we're too *far* away from the rest of the world?
Yes.
We are where a normal human would never survive.
Exactly.
A human would never come here. You have to earn your place here.
Yes.
But Magda, by doing so...it feels, somewhat, like we've removed ourselves from society.
We're building a new society. Just like you said.
Yes, yes...
But...
It's one thing to fantasize about it, it's another to write about it, but now that we're here, the real thing...
There's something I never told you Charles...
My parents were Canadian Weapon X agents.
Canadian...
Where they found the first mutant? You were *there?*
Yes.
I was born into a relatively normal life.
Then I turned thirteen...and I made the silverware dance.
So my father got drunk as he could and tried to kill me.

He pulled his gun on me.
But I turned the bullet around in midair and sent it back to him.
Without even realizing I was doing it.
Just--
--a defense mechanism.

And it was that day that I learned what my parents did for a living.
Where I lived.
I broke into their labs and freed that "Mutant X."

The rumors are true, Charles. They were doing experiments on him.
All day. Every day...for decades. Right under my nose.
They were seeing what would happen to him if they did this or that.
I freed that mutant. My first one.
I *freed* him.

My mother tried to stop me.
She *died* trying to stop me.
But that mutant was freed.
And I knew then that *this* was my life's work.
To set us free. One by one if I had to. But all of us.
He was the first.

Mutant X?
Will he come here?

No, Charles. His path is his own. He's welcome here anytime...
He knows that.
But to take him out of a prison and to make him stay here if he didn't want to--put him into another one.
That is not what this is about.

My point is--and as my parents illustrated to me...
The reason we're here and not *there* is the humans are simply not *ready* for us yet.
They *will* be. Eventually. Maybe even in our lifetime.

One thing at a time, Charles.
Today is about us.
In your head is your dream school.
You've dreamt it. You've fantasized about it down to the very last detail, right?
Let *me* see it.

Put it in *my* head.
Show me your vision of the world.

But not now.
You know this. You as much as said it.

I said: Education of mutants is *part* of it...
Education of the *human* masses is another.

Okay.

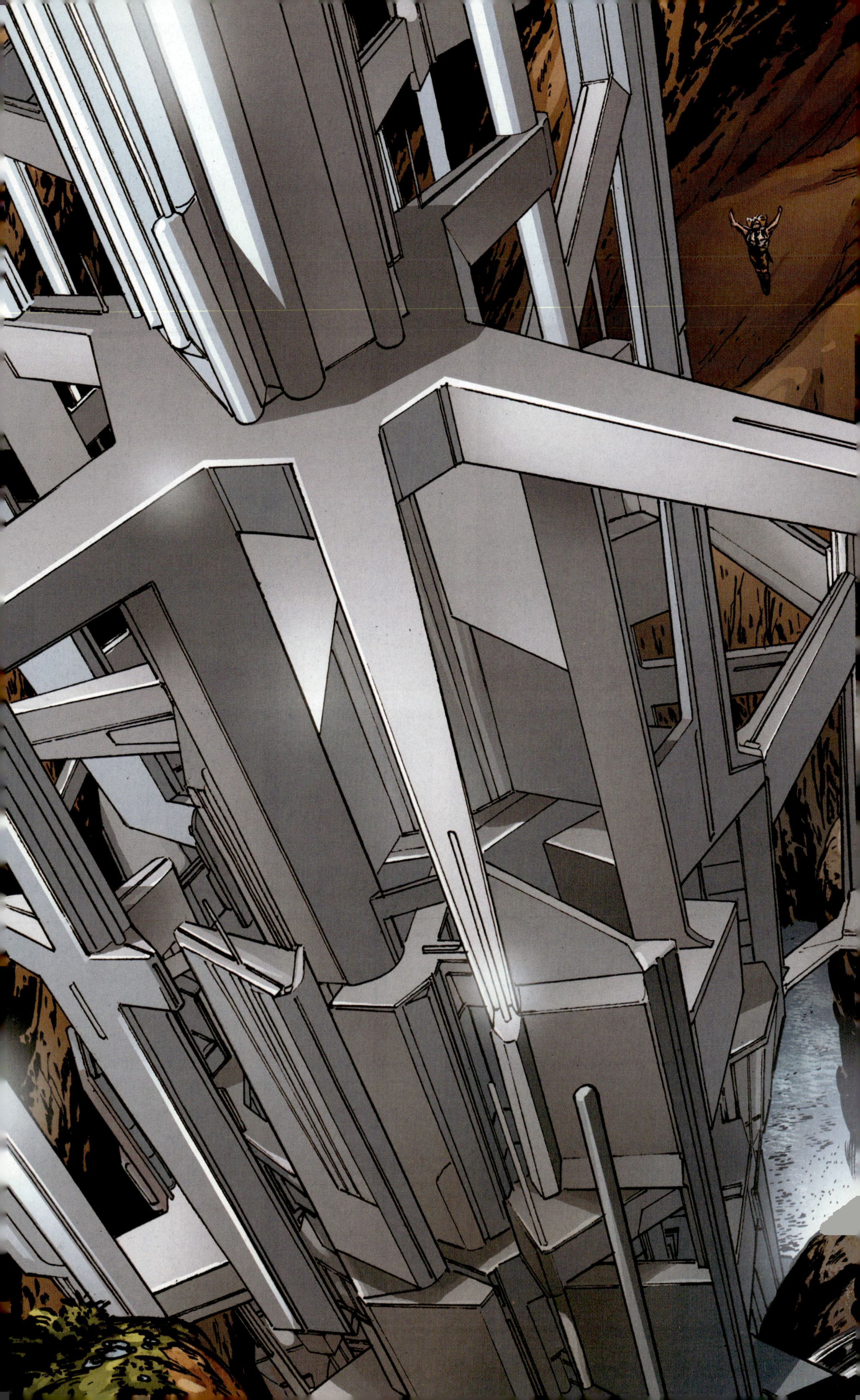

One thing at a time.

Kuwait, Years Ago.
"Do you know how you got here, Fury? Has anyone told you?
"Weapon X--Wolverine--carried you on his back, across the deserts of Kuwait, and brought you to us.
"It's true.
"A filthy, mutant, killing machine saved you.
"All that animal is programmed to do is kill. And yet he saved you.
"Now if I was a thinking man, I would have to take pause and reflect on this.
"The nature of man, war, and all that...
"But I'm not.
"Instead I'm going to focus my thoughts on you."

I'm Thaddeus Ross. I just made General in this man's army.
And you, you're Nick Fury, war hero.
Nick Fury, soldier of fortune, turned black ops commando.
Nick Fury.
And if I dig a little further on you, I bet I would find that up until five years ago Nick Fury did not exist.
هاده وارد
المكثفة
قسم العنايه
Sure I did, general.
I'm here, ain't I?
Yes, you are. *Sure*, you are.
But where were you before?
Don't answer, hotshot. I dug.
Yeah, sure... you're a war hero *now*.
But way back in World War II, Nick Fury had kind of a spotty record.

This *is* you, right?
This ain't your daddy or your grandpappy. This is you.
I wouldn't ask something so plainly silly as to why you could be ninety-something years old and look as good as you do...
ULTRA-EYES ONLY
FURY, NICHOLAS J.
001373-A
...if not for the fact that you came in here *yesterday* holding your own guts and today it looks like you're ready to walk the hell out of here.
Well, minus the eye.

Your file--your World War II record says you got tossed in the clink.
Says you died there.
But it's a red file and stamped and sealed top secret...
FAP

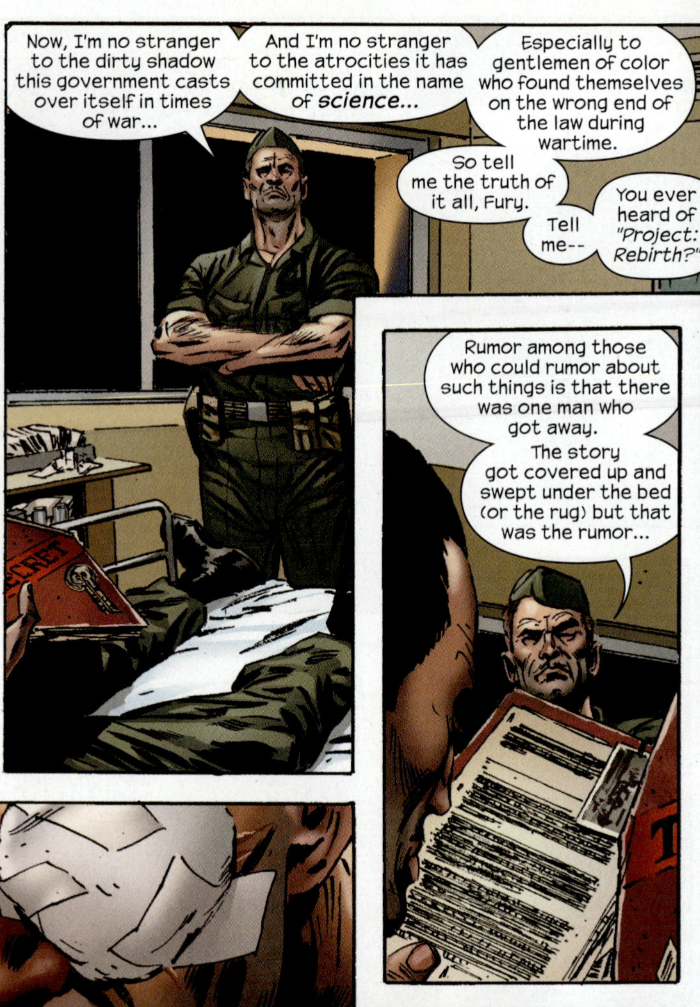

Now, I'm no stranger to the dirty shadow this government casts over itself in times of war...
And I'm no stranger to the atrocities it has committed in the name of science...
Especially to gentlemen of color who found themselves on the wrong end of the law during wartime.
So tell me the truth of it all, Fury.
Tell me--
You ever heard of "Project: Rebirth?"
Rumor among those who could rumor about such things is that there was one man who got away.
The story got covered up and swept under the bed (or the rug) but that was the rumor...
Were you the one that got away?
And if so, why'd you come back to us?

Why are you running around the desert lookin' to get your head blown off?
Why are you using your real name?
You call yourself Chucky Furystein this conversation never had to happen.

It's the name my momma gave me.
It's the only thing they couldn't take.

Or, deep down, you wanted to be found out.
But I really want to know, of all the places in the world you could be...
Why did you come back on duty?

You got it all right.
They took me and made me a super-soldier guinea pig without even asking and didn't care if I lived or died.
And *that* is some heinous @#$%.
Thing is, I lived.
I blamed *everyone* for what happened.
White people, German people, the President, Captain America, Albert Einstein.

You name it, I blamed 'em.
And you walk around the world long enough, you suddenly realize things...
It occurred to me, that maybe--just maybe--I had a little something to do with the situation I found myself in.
I *let* them do this to me.

I was the one who was acting the fool and got myself arrested during the war.
I'm the one who set the wheels a-turning.
No one else.
I swore to serve this country and instead I @#$ed it up.
I went back on my word as a man.
It took me a while to realize it, but, all this, it's a second chance.
Almost a do-over.

So I said to myself: Okay, I'll do it over.
I reenlisted and I'm doing my best every day to do better than I did before.
And yeah, maybe this ain't the great war--
--but as I recall, *that* war wasn't all that great, either.
You know what happens *now*, though...

Word's gonna get out. People are going to want to talk to you.
Guess so.
The President is very interested in reinstating the Super-Soldier program.
No @#$%.
Or a version of it. He believes the next great war will be a genetic war.
SECRET

He's right, and it'll be against the mutants.

Yep.
And, brother, you are going to be his favorite toy in the whole world.

We'll see.

We'll see?
Fury. If you're really the first true Captain America, then why don't you be the first true Captain America?

I ain't him.
There's only one Captain America and he died in the war.

Maybe back in the day they thought a black man couldn't wear the flag, but--

It *ain't* about that.
I *ain't* Captain America.

You're the closest thing we got.
I'm not being modest.

There's a certain type of man that can represent an ideal to a nation and a world, and I have lived long enough and gained enough wisdom to know I am **not** that man.
I'm the guy who ran away.

That being said, you will be summoned.
And the question will be: Fury, you gonna run away or are you gonna offer us something?
What are you gonna offer the world?

One Year Later.
Dover, New Jersey.
Morning.
I met the President last week and he told me he wanted a new Captain America.
A Super-Soldier.
Then maybe a *thousand* of them.
I told him what he needed to do.
I told him he needed to get the best brains money could buy and get them working on it exclusively.
He said he *did* do that.
And I said, no he didn't. Clearly.
I said, you let me go headhunt for you and see if I can't hunt some heads.
I told him he needs to get the guys I pick and put them all in a room together.
One of those rooms with a lot of expensive stuff.
And then get them to work on securing our future as a nation and as a species.
And here you are.
Doctor Franklin Storm, meet Richard Parker.
Richard Parker, meet Doctor Bruce Banner.
Bruce Banner meet--
Our intern?
Intern?
What's 3,424,235, 235,345 x 2, 352,532?
Um.
Don't know your gazintas? Then *you* get the coffee, pappy.
This is Hank Pym.
Just graduated MIT. For the second time.
Let it go.
Intern my--*OW!*

Super-Soldier program.
Yes.
Can we see the *original* project files?
No.
No?
They were destroyed.
They were?
Long ago.
Why?
I'll tell you when I get to know you better.

Then we're starting from scratch?
No.
There's this...

Is--is this Captain America's blood?
No. But examine it. Reverse engineer it. Do what you do.
Where did this come from?

Get crackin' or it's all our asses.
Oh, and one thing. No human testing.
None.
What-so-ever.
Well, at some point--

At *no* point.
How are we supposed to make a Super-Soldier with no soldiers to make super?

We'll deal with that when we deal with it.

Super-Soldier.

Today.

Are we being invaded?
Who would *want* to?
Seriously.

That was before the others started popping up, Johnny. This is a *thing* now.
I still feel we should be covering our privates.
No. We have to find a way to communicate with it.
I think I should hit it.
Hey guys. I said I want essential personnel *only*. I want everyone out of *here!!*
Lockdown!!
But, Captain Danvers, do you understand, we have very sensitive material in here that--

There are *more* of these things?
Popping up all over.
How *many* more?
I don't know. Reports are coming in. Baxter Building, Triskelion, Ultimates' Mansion...
I think you were right before, Ben.
I think--I think it is observing us. I think it wants to communicate.
Hey Reed, didn't we just, five minutes ago, run out of here covering our privates in fear of alien radiation?
What happened to *that?*

Colonel or-or Captain--
Sergeant Vaughn.
Sergeant, this--that thing. It's been sitting there for decades.
That is our understanding.
Someone put it there.
Someone knows exactly what that thing is.
Find out.

15 Years Ago.
Give me an update on *Project: Rebirth Two*, Fury.
It's coming along, Mister President.
Is that French for *"you're jerking me around?"*
No, sir, I say what I mean. It's coming along.
They seem up. Involved. They're in the right headspace. Banner in particular. I don't think the man sleeps.
Okay then.
RESULT: NEGATIVE
I will say, sir, that letting the Army poach Doctor Storm out from under me for your Baxter Building project didn't help us in any--
Sorry about that, Fury, what can I say--I have many fish to fry--
BRUCE-
I THOUGH
PYM WA
THE IDIO
I understand, but if you are sincere in this initiative, we have to keep the team intact and--
If you find someone else who can replace him, you have the money to do it.
I'm going to see what they do first; if we need fresh blood we'll get some.
I still say, Howard Stark and that boy of his.
NEGATIVE
No. No. Now that Parker is back from his leave--
Where did he leave to? He's supposed to be working on a top secret--
His wife had a baby, I gave him a couple of weeks.
So when do I get to *see* something?
I promise, when I have something to show, you'll be the first person I show it to.
I'm not a fan of sass, Fury. I'm a fan of getting the job done.
Yes, sir.
NEGATIVE

Guys...
I think I have it.
You don't have it.
Let me see.

It's--it's interesting, Bruce.
You don't have it.
You're not even looking, Parker.
You *want* to have it. Doesn't mean you *do.*
It doesn't look *bad.*
Print it out. I'll read it.

We should get some dogs and cats and do some testing.
Show it to Fury.
Or show it to Fury.
Show it to Fury?
If we show it to Fury, he will take it and hand it off to Army scientists and we'll never see the end of this and never get the credit and we'll never get the--

No, he won't.
Oh, yes he will.
This is *his* project.
And it's not his only project. The man is working all kinds of angles on this.
Who told you *that?* Your girlfriend?

Betty knows how the military works.

Hey, between me and you, scale of one to ten, how sure are you this works?
Damn sure.
You want to test it?
On who?
On *me.*
On you?
No. No, kid.

Why not?

Seriously. I want it.

I'll do it. Me first.
You spot me.

Yeah okay.

Parker's out of the building. He's gone.
Good, okay, Check the low gate.
Did. We're gold.
Are you recording?
Hell, yes. They can show it while we pick up our Nobels.

Hey, Mrs. Parker!
You read my mind. Because I wanted to see you guys.
Oh, does he? Did he say that?
Your son wanted to see his daddy, *Mister* Parker.
Peter wants to see where you work.
A mother can tell.

Okay.
AGH!
It's in.

I was thinking about buying those bikes.
Definitely.
I gotta get back in shape.
Let's do it.

How do you feel?

BOOM
What was that?

What the hell happened in there?
It's--! Don't!
NO!!
What happened??!!

Go to the car!!
What happened?
Go to the CAR!!

What- what did you--?

SCRACH
Richard?

HUUAARRGGHH!!
SHRAKATHH
AAAIIEE!!!
TANG
Nnn...
N-not...

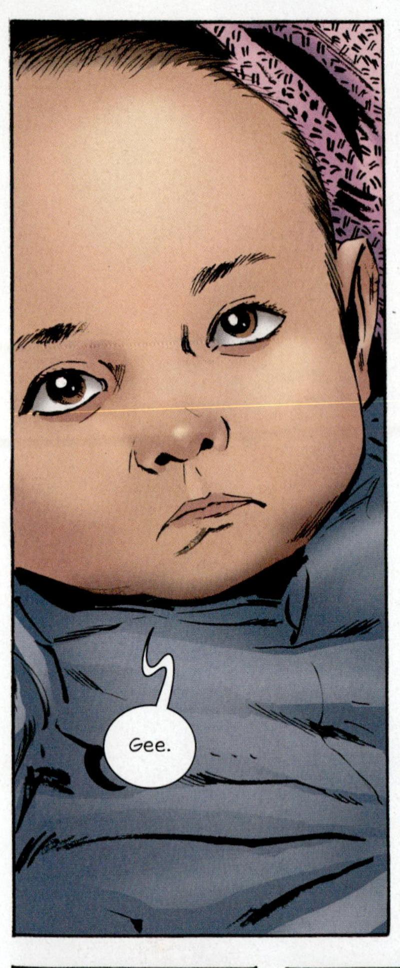
Gee.

No...

No...

I didn't mean to--

CRACK

What did you do??
WHAT DID YOU DO??!!

What did you do?
Gafa!

Hey, little guy.
I swear to you, kid. This wasn't supposed to happen this way.
Flah!
People get a little crazy.
The good news is, you're so young...
...you won't remember *any* of this.

Today.
Tony Stark, this is Reed Richards. Can you hear me clearly?
I hear you. What have you got?
I have an obelisk of alien design and indeterminate material.

It seems to have activated itself. It could be either biological or inanimate. I can't tell.
Hey, that's exactly what I have over here.
Have you made any contact with it?
Thor hit it. It did nothing.
I've done a full scan--it just bounces back.

Well, I want a full ladvun scan off the decon server. Do you have a---
It watches.

What?

It is a Watcher.
It is part of a hive culture that is here to observe and record the significant events that shape our civilization.
It is here now to witness the most significant event of this generation.
It just told me--
It is here to witness the coming devastation.

WHITE

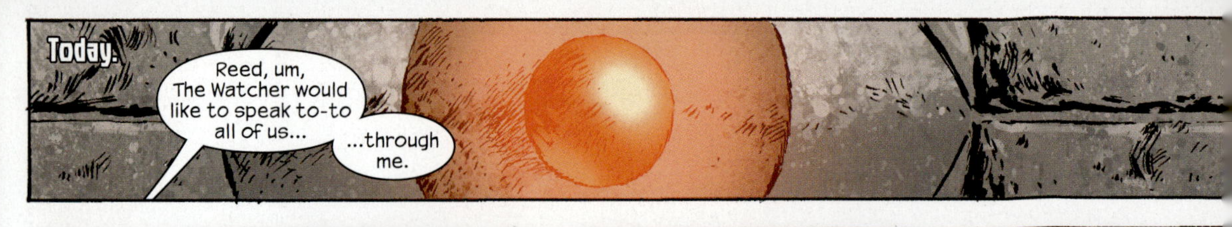
Today.
Reed, um, The Watcher would like to speak to-to all of us...
...through me.

Project Pegasus.
And it's asking you if it's okay?

Yes.

(That's rather polite.)
For a rock thing from wherever.
I don't like this.
You can hear it in your head?
Clear as I can hear you.
What's it saying NOW, Susie?
S.H.I.E.L.D., This is Danvers, we may have a situation, hold for command.

It says it won't harm me.
Or any of us.

Do, hmmm, do you *want* to do this?
Well...
It's your call, I guess.
I think it'll be okay. I really do.
And as your brother, may I say, I don't like any part of this.

My name is Uatu.
I am a Watcher.

How long have you been watching us?
For many years.
Why?
That is our species design.
Why are you making yourself known to us now? Why here?
We have made ourselves known to you before.
You seemed to lack the capacity to understand our true meaning.
Many of us have been destroyed by your species.
But we understand the concept of fear. We are not offended. That is not our design.
This place represents everything we have observed and it is time for you to rediscover this history.
You spoke of devastation.
Yes.
That is coming to us. To Earth.

Yes.
In what form?
We cannot say.
Cannot or will not?
We would tell you if we knew.
Then how do you know it is coming?
We have observed many critical moments in your recent history.
Moments whose true meanings are about to converge with one another.

What moments?

The birth of heroes. The birth of a new species.
Your species just NOW taking responsibility for the science it has discovered.
All these things plus so many more.
Your wars, your passions, your plagues, your emotions...
Understanding. Misunderstanding.
We have observed all of it. From afar and up close.
We have witnessed this from not only your world but countless other worlds of similar design and model.
And we now know that your devastation is coming.

So you're guessing... you don't know for sure.

It is our design to know.
Johnny, please stop arguing with the advanced alien life form.
(You're embarrassing me.)
Yeah okay.
Uatu, what will you do with this information?
Yeah, what? You're just gonna sit around and watch us destroy ourselves?

No.
We will now pick a herald to help you with your new world order.
A herald?
A herald of what?
One who will harness the power needed for such a task.
Who will this herald be?

We will choose now.

Weapon X. Alberta, Canada. Years Ago.
Alpha team, positions.
First positions clear.
Okay kids. This is it.
This is Weapon X.
Assassin training camp and all-around illegal bit of Canadian business.
Weapons up and get ready for a firefight. The intel on this joint is these are the nastiest of the nasty so this is a "shoot first" situation.
Canadians, Fury? Really?
Kicking a Canadian in the tush don't seem all that professional.
Well, Dugan...
BOOM
I'm sure you'll get over it.

What- what is the *meaning of this?*
Oh no... oh no...
Uh...
This ain't no training camp.
The hell?

Who the-??
And who the hell are you?

Nick Fury, Director of S.H.I.E.L.D.
You monsters are under arrest!!!
SPOK

Really? Under what authority?
Mine.
You get on the ground. You put your hands on your heads.
Enjoy your moment, soldier!

Who the hell is he supposed to be?
Malcolm Colcord. Doctor Malcolm Colcord!
GRAAGGH!
Whoa!
Yo, Fury, what do we do with these things?
Is it human?
I wouldn't touch that.

He'll kill you as soon as look at you.
You have no right!! We're scientists and--
You made them this way? You? You did this?

We created new life. What have *you* done?
I'm going to enjoy watching you try to figure out what has happened to your career as I am embraced by your government's science community.

(Deluded...)
I helped create a new species.

New species of what?

Homo superior!!
Mutants. We created them.
Right here. We did it. It's all here.
And when I show the community what we've done, and what we're on the cusp of discovering now...
If you think they are going to toss me in a prison then you don't know your history, my friend...
Man created mutants?
And what have you done?
BAM

NO!!!
Nooo!!
What did you do??!!

Burn it.
Everything and everyone.

You sure?
If the world ever finds out what went on in this place...
If mutants ever find out...
If the world ever finds out that man invented mutants...
The entire Earth will burn.
You heard the man. Go to black!! Clean it!
Full sweep!!
NO!!
BLAM BLAM BLAM

What's your name, son?

Chart says T'Challa Udaku.

What do you want to do, Fury?

NNYAAAGH!

You're coming with me, now.

Savage Land,
Years Ago.

AAAGGH!!
I love you, Charles.

I am your friend and your brother.
And you are the greatest mutant I have ever met.
The greatest.
Your teachings opened my eyes.
None of what I have accomplished would have happened without your vision.
We're at war with the humans.
I take no joy in that. I take no pleasure in it.
But do understand we were put in a war the day you were born.
And they are the ones that put you there.
Not me.
So you either choose to win this war and live free, or you choose to let them enslave you.
Torture you.
Kill you.
Education??
You thought the answer was education??
Did you use education to defy me??
Did you use education to challenge me??
See, Charles, I was willing to wait as long as it took.
I was willing to wait for you to gain the life experience of their hatred and racism...
I was willing to wait for you to see it the way I do.
The way we all do, on your own.
But instead I get Charles the hypocrite.
Using his powers to get inside my head.
Attacking me in my own home.
What would you have done next?

You'll send them here??
The humans??
And we'd kill them.
All you would have done is give them a reason to come round the mutants up.
You'd plant another seed of hate and you'll see exactly how they react and you'll see no matter what your feelings on the subject are...
You'll see that I'm right!!
That humans and mutants cannot live together in peace.
God has selected the mutant as the dominant species on the planet!!!!
God did this!!
It's his will!!
AND WHO ARE YOU TO DEFY IT!!??

God created me.
And his will be done.
No matter what the cost.

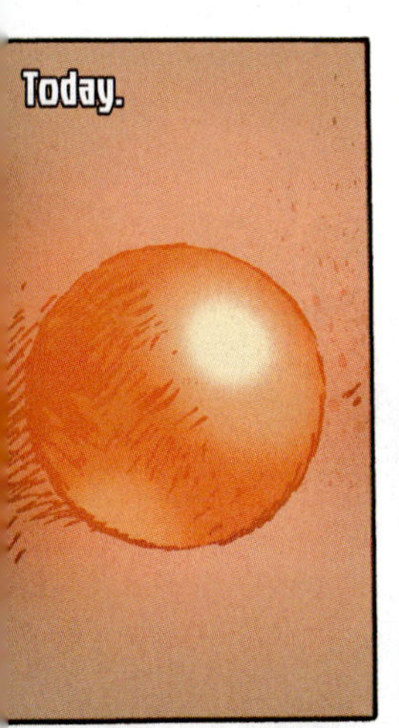
Today.

What's happening now?
(I don't know.)
I hate when you don't know.

The herald has been chosen.

Who is it?
Is it me?

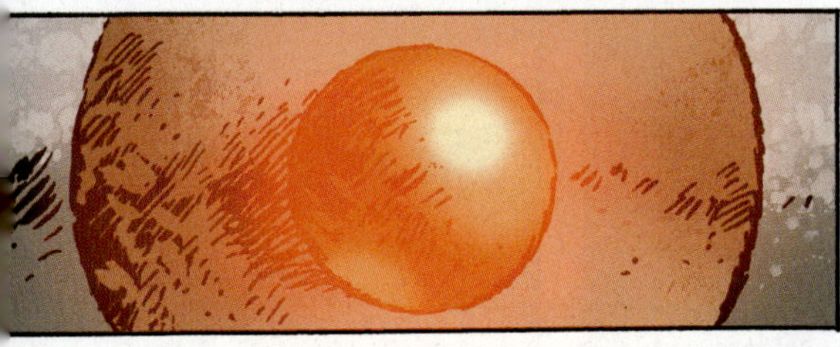

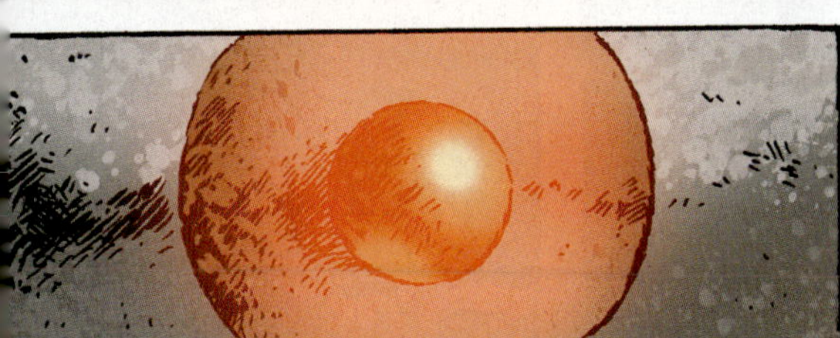

Ugh!
Are you okay?
I- I- I think so.
Hello?? Is this thing on??

What happened?
One of us?
They picked a herald.
This is Danvers. Yeah, what?

Okay, the other Watchers just up and disappeared.
Yeah, so did ours.

So... who is it?
Who'd they pick?

Midwestern U.S.
RICK JONES!!

Rick? Dinner!
Rick??
BE DIFFERENT

Where is your brother?
Backyard.

Rick!

Rick?

The End.

1 Variant by Michael Turner

1 Wizard World Chicago Variant Cover by Joe Quesada

1 Dynamic Forces Variant Cover by Howard Chaykin